BEHIND THE BORDER

When school began again in September, our teacher, Maria Petrovna, had a big talk with us. She told us how careful we had to be if we ever met a foreigner. "Some foreigners make believe they're your best friends, but you must be wise and remember that they're enemies of the Soviet people," she said. "You should never accept gifts from foreigners. Many Russian children who accepted candy from foreigners are dead now, because these foreigners hid tiny bombs in the candy. After the children ate the candy, they got blown up."

I held my breath and thought of the candy I'd been given by Karl and Monika. I'd eaten it only two days earlier. Something turned in my stomach. This is the end, I thought. I'm going to be blown up. I wanted to raise my hand and ask how many days the bomb would take to explode. But I was ashamed of being unwise and of accepting gifts from foreigners. I didn't hear anything else the teacher said that day. I was preparing to explode.

BEHIND THE BORDER

BEHIND THE BORDER

BY NINA KOSSMAN

A BEECH TREE PAPERBACK BOOK  NEW YORK

The Library of Congress has cataloged the
Lothrop, Lee & Shepard Books edition of *Behind the
Border* as follows:
Kossman, Nina.
Behind the border: memories of a Russian
childhood/Nina Kossman.
p. cm.
ISBN 0-688-13494-7
[1. Kossman, Nina—Childhood and youth—Juvenile
literature.
2. Soviet Union—Biography.] I. Title.
CT1218.K54A3 1994 947.085′082—dc20 [B]
93-48617 CIP AC

10 9 8 7 6 5 4 3 2 1
First Beech Tree Edition, 1996
ISBN 0-688-14742-9

FOR MY PARENTS,
AND FOR ANDY, WITH THANKS.
THANKS ALSO TO JUDIT BODNAR.
N.K.

CONTENTS

UNTIL RECENTLY, VERY FEW PEOPLE WERE ALLOWED TO LEAVE THE FORMER SOVIET UNION, OR EVEN TO VISIT OTHER COUNTRIES. TRAVELING TO ANOTHER COUNTRY WAS CALLED GOING BEHIND THE BORDER.

WHAT HAPPENED TO THE BEACH BALL

The summer when I was five, we went to the Black Sea. We stayed in Sochi, a sea town. Every day we went to the beach. We swam in the sea and lay in the sun. My brother, Misha, and I played with a beach ball my father had brought us from his trip. Very few Soviet children had a beach ball like this: it was bright red, blue, and yellow; you could let the air out of it, and you could blow it up again.

One day we were playing with the ball in the water. When I threw it to Misha, a wave carried it away from us. He tried to swim after it, but it floated away, farther and farther. Finally it was so far away, it looked like just a dot out in the sea. All the people at the beach were watching it. Someone said, "That ball is on its way to Turkey now."

"Where is Turkey?" I asked my mother when I was drying out in the sun.

"Turkey is behind the border," my mother said. "You can't go there."

My father had brought us the beach ball from behind the border, and now the beach ball was going back there. Behind the border must have been like a home for beach balls. They couldn't stay away from it for too long, just as I didn't like to be away from my mom and dad.

Somebody at the beach let us look through special glasses — binoculars; they made everything far away look nearer. We could see our red, blue, and yellow ball still jumping on the waves.

"Maybe the beach ball is getting lost on its way to Turkey," I said.

"Would you like to show it the right way to go, Nina?" Misha said, and he laughed at me.

"Maybe I would," I said stubbornly.

On our way back into town, we passed a ferryboat that was getting ready to cruise along the shoreline. I ran toward a man who was standing next to it. He wore a white cap; he was a sailor.

"Wait!" I shouted. "Can you take me over to Turkey?"

"Turkey? You can't go over to Turkey. It's behind the border." He looked at me strangely. "Why do you want to go to Turkey?"

"Because my beach ball is swimming over to Turkey. It may get there this very night," I said.

"I'm sorry. I can't help you," the sailor said, shrugging his shoulders. "We are not allowed to go behind the border."

My father came up, took my hand, and said to the man in the white cap, "Please excuse my little girl, officer. She doesn't know what she's saying."

Back home my parents told me to stop talking about Turkey to strangers. "You may get us into trouble," they said.

When my brother and I were left alone in the kitchen, I said, "If nobody can talk about going behind the border to get my beach ball, can we dig out a tunnel and go there at night? Nobody will see us. We'll go in on this side of the tunnel, and we'll get out on the other side."

"By the time you dig a tunnel like that, our beach ball will be so far over into Turkey that nobody will ever find it for us," Misha said.

"How long does it take to dig a tunnel?"

"Many years," he said.

I sighed. What could we do? I felt as if my beach ball were calling to me. I wanted to find a way to get it back.

"There shouldn't be any borders at all!" I said. "Then anybody could go behind the border and get a beach ball back."

"How would you get rid of borders?" my brother asked, laughing at me again. Then he took out a map and showed me the borders of our country and the nearby countries.

"This is how." I picked up a pencil eraser that was on the table. "I'll just erase all these borders, so the whole world will be all together. Nothing to separate countries. No more wars and no more problems."

"I wish it were as simple as that," my father said as he came into the kitchen.

He promised to get me another beach ball, but that

15

didn't make me any happier. I didn't want another beach ball. I wanted my old one. Every night when I went to sleep that summer, I could see it jumping on the waves like an awkward seal, calling to me, pleading with me to save it, my poor red, blue, and yellow ball, lost in the sea between two countries.

WAKING LENIN

Like every child in Russia, I loved Lenin. We believed that Lenin was a grandfather to all Russian children. We believed we should love him even more than we loved our mothers and fathers. I loved Lenin, but I knew that I loved my mother and father much more. I felt so guilty about not loving Lenin as much as I should that for a while I did not even kiss my parents good night.

One day our kindergarten teacher announced that we were going to visit Lenin's tomb. People from all over the Soviet Union went to look at Lenin lying there.

I had a great idea.

I decided to wake Lenin. When our kindergarten group got close enough to Lenin, I would bend over him and open his eyes. He would sit up and say, "Thank you for waking me, Ninotchka. I've been lying here too long." I would become a national heroine, I thought. My picture would be in all the newspapers. People would point at me in the street and say, "Here's the brave girl who woke Lenin."

Every morning my father took me to kindergarten by trolley bus. We paid our fare and got our ticket. If one of the numbers was a five, you had a lucky ticket. To get all that luck into your life, to make it all your own, you had to eat your ticket. For seven days before our trip to see Lenin, I ate all my lucky tickets. I hoped all this luck would help me wake Lenin.

Finally the day arrived, and the moment came. I had a bad stomachache, but there I was, standing in line at Lenin's Tomb with my best friend, Lena M.

Lenin was lying on a large black bed. There were

guards on all four sides of him. Each guard held up a long rifle with a bayonet. I took Lena's hand as we filed closer. Lenin was covered with a big glass dome. How could I open his eyes?

Still, I had to do something. I stepped a little closer, but Lena was afraid and she held me back by the button of my coat. I pulled away from her, and the button popped off and rolled under Lenin's bed. As I ran to get my button, the guards shouted, "That's not allowed!" and they pushed me away. I was frightened. How could Grandfather Lenin let them do this to me?

So I did not get to wake Lenin, not even with all my lucky tickets. After the guards pushed me out, I no longer believed that Lenin was a grandfather to all Russian children. I started kissing my mother and father good night again because I knew there was nothing wrong with loving them more than Lenin.

TULA

My friend Masha had a problem in kindergarten. Her parents had to get up many times every night because Masha wet her bed. Masha's mother looked very tired every morning when she brought Masha in. Masha's parents asked our teacher what to do. "We can't go on like this, without sleep," they said.

The next day, Nadezhda Osipovna — the director of our kindergarten — gathered us together for a special talk. She showed us something that looked like a golden shoestring and said, "This is a magic cord from a special TV. This TV shows me what each of you does at home. You children must behave well, not just at school but also at home. You must try to be mature day and night; you aren't babies anymore." We knew she was talking about Masha and her problem. She said there'd be a lot of trouble if her golden-cord TV showed us acting like babies at home. "If this kind of behavior goes on," she said, "I'll have to take measures."

We all knew what the worst of these measures was. It was being sent to Tula, where monsters lived who scared little children. Tula was a town somewhere near Moscow. But we didn't know it was not so far; to us, it seemed like the farthest place on earth. We were so afraid of being sent to Tula that we couldn't hear the word without trembling.

For several days after that talk, we lived in fear of the TV with the golden cord. We went to bed when we were told; we were perfect. I don't know if Masha still wet her bed, but we could all see that Masha's mother didn't look so tired anymore. This lasted only a few days. Then Masha's mother had another talk with our teacher and with Nadezhda Osipovna, the director. Masha cried all day. She didn't want to talk to anybody, not even to me. But I was her friend, and of course I guessed what had happened: she'd wet her bed again, and now she was afraid that she'd be sent to Tula.

This is not right, I thought. Why should poor Masha be punished for something she can't help doing? Why should we all be so afraid of being sent to Tula? Does Nadezhda Osipovna really have a special TV with a golden cord, or does she just make that up to scare us? In the evening I asked my mother, "Is there such a thing as a TV that would let one person spy on another at home?"

My mother said, "I've never heard of such a thing." Now I knew it was all just a bluff.

The next day I said to the other kids, "You shouldn't be afraid of getting sent away to Tula. The special TV with the golden cord doesn't exist." I told them these were just threats, and that it was not very nice of Nadezhda Osipovna to scare us in this way.

The others agreed with me, even though some still thought there was something to the story of Tula and the special TV. But we were no longer afraid. The next time Nadezhda Osipovna started telling us that story, we just looked at her. One girl giggled. Nadezhda Osipovna asked the girl what the matter was, and the girl said, "Nina told us you don't have any special TV with a golden cord."

That day I was called into Nadezhda Osipovna's office. I hadn't been there since the first day, when my mother brought me to kindergarten. I was afraid, but when Nadezhda Osipovna asked me, "Are you spreading rumors against me?" I said yes. She again showed me that golden cord from her special TV.

"But it's just a shoestring! There is no special TV! You're a liar!" I shouted. "My friend Masha is crying all the time because of your lies!"

Nadezhda Osipovna telephoned my mother at work. "Please take your daughter to a doctor," she said.

"What happened?" asked my mother.

"Your daughter has been spreading rumors against our staff here. She is in my office now, saying unspeakable things to me."

So my mother took me to a special doctor, a psychiatrist. The doctor said, "There is nothing wrong with this little girl or her mind." When I went back to the kindergarten, Nadezhda Osipovna no longer threatened us with Tula or with her golden-cord TV. We tried to behave well even though we knew we weren't going to be sent away. And I liked her a little better this way, without her lies.

FOOD

Maybe I was a bad eater in general, or maybe I just didn't like the food in the Soviet Union. It was a big country, but the people there didn't have much to eat, and what they had didn't taste too good.

At home, dinner was always the same, either chicken soup or farina. To get rid of them, I hid chicken wings in the closet in my grandma's room. Nobody knew my secret for a long time. Only when we were moving to a different apartment did my parents discover the old chicken bones, the source of the mysterious bad smell.

Hot cereal was more difficult to get rid of. My mother set a bowl of farina in front of me and put a clock next to it. She said, "I'm leaving the kitchen now," and pointed at the minute hand. "I'll be back when this hand reaches six. I want all the farina in this bowl eaten by then." Alone, I looked at the bowl, and I knew there was no way I could eat all that farina. It was so white and mushy. Disgusting.

One day I had an idea. I stood on a chair, opened a cupboard, took out a can, and poured some ground coffee into the farina. Then I poured in some salt, some pepper, and some vinegar. I added a little mustard and stirred it all up. When the minute hand reached six, my mother came back in.

"Why haven't you finished your farina?"

"But, Mama, how can anyone eat this? Try it yourself!"

At school, too, food was a torture. We had breakfast every day in kindergarten. I spent hours finishing it. You weren't allowed to leave the table until your plate was clean. The longer I sat at that table, the colder my breakfast got. I tried all sorts of tricks to get rid of the food without eating it. I might keep it in my cheek and then spit it out into the toilet later. But I couldn't always manage that, because we went to the toilet only in groups of five or six, and I was afraid of getting caught. Sometimes I sat at the table all day. I missed playtime; I fell asleep with pieces of food hidden in my cheeks.

Once, instead of scrambled eggs, the usual breakfast, they gave us each a piece of bread with red jam. The bread was so hard that my teeth got tired chewing it. The jam stuck to my teeth. When nobody was looking, I hid the piece of bread in my underpants. I thought, Nobody can guess where I've hidden my breakfast.

I was allowed to leave the table and play with the other kids. At first the jam sticking to my stomach bothered me, but soon I forgot about it. Later in the day, when my mother took me home, she saw something was not quite right. "Take out whatever it is you've put in your underpants!" She saw that it was a sandwich. "Now tell me, Ninotchka, who put that there?"

I said I didn't know. She asked me again, and suddenly I came out with a lie. "It was Sasha Yashkov," I said.

My mother turned pale when she heard this. She telephoned my father at work, and they talked for a half hour. Then my mother said to me, "Your father is going to speak to the teacher about this Sasha Yashkov."

The next day my father came in to see the teacher. "There must be something wrong with this boy Sasha Yashkov. Why does he put his jam sandwiches in little girls' underpants?"

The teacher replied, "I don't believe Sasha would do that. Sasha's a very good eater, and he would never, ever give away his food. Ask Nina. Maybe she did it herself. We all know she doesn't like to eat."

At home my mother said to me, "Just think, Ninotchka. Maybe Sasha Yashkov didn't do anything. Maybe you put the jam sandwich there yourself? How will you feel if he gets punished for nothing?"

"Rotten," I mumbled.

"So?" said my mother. I turned away from her, hid my head in the sofa.

"I did it," I said at last.

I was glad Sasha never learned about what happened. He remained my friend and often helped me by secretly eating food off my plate.

WHO'S DIFFERENT?

There were two Lenas in my grade. Lena M. was my best friend; Lena S., my worst enemy. Maybe Lena S. was jealous of my friendship with Lena M. If she said to Lena M., "How come Nina is your best friend?" Lena M. would answer, "Just because she is."

Lena S. always did things to spite me. One time a new teacher came to our class and said:

"Here in Moscow, as in the whole Soviet Union, all people are equal. Our government cares for everybody, no matter what the person's nationality. Here in this class, we have not only real Russian children but also some Jews. They have the same rights as everybody else. How many Jews do you have in your class?" the teacher asked Katya T.

Katya, our class leader, looked at the floor. She turned red. "I don't know. I never counted them."

"Count them now," the teacher said. "Jews, raise your hands."

Several children raised their hands. They held their hands up only for a second, then put them down quickly. They blushed and looked around to see if the rest of the class was looking at them. I was scared and I didn't even put up my hand.

Then Lena S. shouted from her desk by the window, "And what about Nina? Why doesn't she raise her hand? She's a Jew, too."

I jumped up from my desk and ran out of the classroom. I was crying. I didn't know what all this was about. I just knew that there was something embarrassing about being a Jew: it was being different from

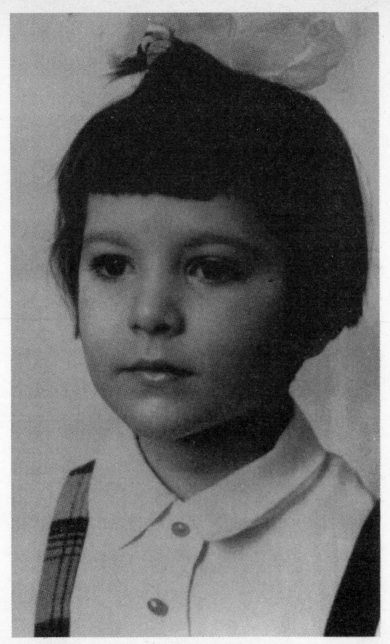

Nina, 5 years old, in the white shirt and plaid skirt required for kindergarten music and dance lessons (1965).

Misha and Nina in the woods near Moscow. Nina is wearing a traditional Russian kerchief.

Misha and Nina in a Moscow park. Misha is holding a newspaper called *Behind the Border*, which presented a Soviet version of what was going on in other countries.

A meal in a kindergarten.

At the Black Sea beach, thinking about the beach ball (1965).

Brother Misha's third-grade class (he is at the far right in the front row), with portrait of Lenin in the background.

Misha with the beach ball, at the Black Sea.

Second grade, with Young Octobrists' star-shaped pins. Nina, age eight, is on the far right in the front row.

First graders at a school play.

On everyone's lap is a set called "First Grader." In it were a pencil, an eraser, a fountain pen, a notebook, and a pencil case. Nina is the one in the checkered dress. The last day of kindergarten.

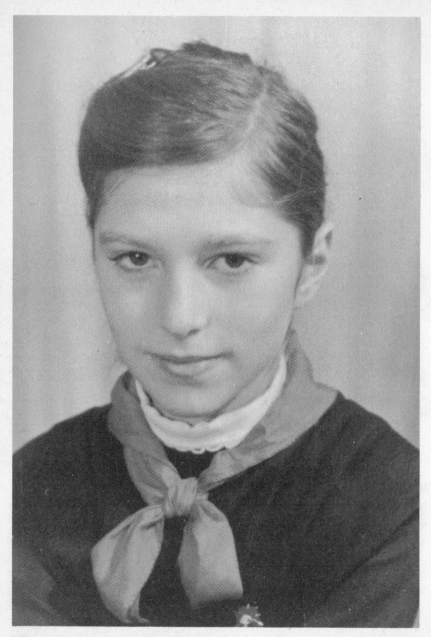

Nina as a Young Pioneer, 4th grade.

everyone else. The teacher came outside to get me to go back to class.

That evening my parents looked sad when I told them about what had happened. I asked, "What is a Jew?"

My mother shook her head and closed her eyes. My father said, "We're Jews. And Jews are like everybody else. All people are the same deep down. You shouldn't believe anyone who tries to make you feel different from everyone else."

Late that night I heard my mother tell my father, "Maybe we should put Nina in a different school. If this kind of thing will go on..." I didn't hear what my father answered.

I kept on going to our school. I just never spoke to Lena S. again. And Lena M. was still my best friend, even if I was a Jew and she wasn't.

FOREIGN GIFTS

I never saw people from another country before the summer I was seven, when I met Karl and Monika on the beach at the Baltic Sea. I was making a sand castle. My parents were sitting in the shade of a big tree not too far off.

I heard my mother calling me. Raising my head, I saw another family spreading a picnic blanket right next to my parents'. At first I thought both of the children in this family were boys, because they were both wearing pants. When I got closer, I realized that one of them was a girl. I was shocked; I had never seen a girl wearing pants.

They were Finns and didn't speak any Russian, so instead of saying anything, I just pointed at my castle.

We built a whole city together, with towers and tunnels and tiny houses. The only words we said were our names: Karl, Monika, Nina. We didn't talk; we built. Monika had a red swimsuit. Karl had red trunks. They looked like twins.

While we were building, I could see that they were chewing something. What could they be chewing? I'd never seen a person chew something for so long. I pointed at my mouth and moved it as if I were chewing; I looked at them and shrugged my shoulders. They laughed. Monika said something to her brother; he ran to the tree and came back with something in his hand. He held it out to me. It looked like a little red ball — some kind of candy. I put it in my mouth and chewed until all the sweetness was gone from it. Then I spit it out. The twins laughed. I didn't know it was chewing gum and you could chew it for a long time.

Before they left, Karl and Monika gave me some more little red balls of chewing gum; they also gave me some Finnish candy to eat later. They never returned to the beach. I spent the rest of my summer chewing gum and thinking of my two Finnish friends in their foreign country. I saved the candy; I didn't eat it till the very last day of summer.

When school began again in September, our teacher, Maria Petrovna, had a big talk with us. She told us how careful we had to be if we ever met a foreigner. "Some foreigners make believe they're your best friends, but you must be wise and remember that they're enemies of the Soviet people," she said. "You should never accept gifts from foreigners. Many Russian children who accepted candy from foreigners are dead now, because these foreigners hid tiny bombs in the candy. After

36

the children ate the candy, they got blown up."

I held my breath and thought of the candy I'd been given by Karl and Monika. I'd eaten it only two days earlier. Something turned in my stomach. This is the end, I thought. I'm going to be blown up. I wanted to raise my hand and ask how many days the bomb would take to explode. But I was ashamed of being unwise and of accepting gifts from foreigners. I didn't hear anything else the teacher said that day. I was preparing to explode.

The next day I had such a stomachache, I couldn't move. My mother took my temperature and made me stay in bed.

"It's all because of that candy," I whispered.

"What?" my mother asked.

"There was a bomb in the candy," I said. "I'm going to be blown up."

"How long ago did you eat that candy?"

"Three days ago."

"Don't worry," my mother said, and she talked to me and held me till I went to sleep.

The next morning I opened my eyes to see if I was still in one piece. My hands, my feet, my nose were just as before. For three more days I waited to be blown up, but nothing happened. Maybe the teacher was wrong after all, and nothing was wrong with the candy Karl and Monika had given me. Or maybe that candy was too small to put a bomb in.

THE RED PIONEER'S TIE

When I was in second grade, everybody in our class was a Young Octobrist. We had buttons with a picture of Lenin as a little boy pinned to the lapels of our school uniforms. We were looking forward to next year. Early in the third grade, some of the best of us would be allowed to become Young Pioneers, who would wear red neckties and pins with pictures of Lenin as a young man, and who would throw their hands up to salute the red flag of the Soviet Union and say "Always ready!" That was the motto of the Young Pioneers. Of course we knew that sooner or later, by fourth grade, we would all be Young Pioneers; but to become one early in the third grade was a great honor, so we worked very hard to earn our red ties.

One day the teacher told us that we would have a contest for the best story. She said we should each bring in a story we wrote at home. Then we'd all decide which story was the best one. The winner of the contest would be accepted into the Young Pioneers next autumn.

When we brought our stories to class on Friday, the teacher read them aloud, without saying who'd written which one. It turned out that the story we all thought was the best was about a white mouse. The white mouse went shopping and had all sorts of interesting adventures on the way.

The teacher announced the name of the winner: Igor Levov.

Igor Levov was sitting at the desk next to mine. He always got good grades for math and bad grades for writing. He said that he wanted to be a scientist, and writing wasn't something a scientist had to be good at. So we were all surprised that Igor Levov would get the first prize for writing a story. The teacher said he would be the first among us to get a Young Pioneer's red tie. Igor looked very happy and pink for several days after the contest. I thought, Maybe he wants to be a writer now.

But soon everything changed for him.

All of us, at home before going to bed, watched a show called "Good Night, Children" on TV. One night they showed a cartoon about a little white mouse who went shopping and had all sorts of interesting adventures along the way. When I saw this cartoon, I thought maybe it wasn't the first time that it had been on TV, and then I thought I knew where Igor's story came from.

The next day in class, I looked at the teacher. Does she know, I wondered. If she didn't know, we weren't going to tell her. We all liked Igor.

At the end of the day, the teacher said, "I have some bad news, children. One of you here is a *plagiarist*." None of us knew what that word meant.

"A plagiarist is a person who takes somebody else's story and shows it off as if he'd written it himself. Now, do you know who is a plagiarist here?" She was looking right at Igor. Igor got red in the face and hid his head behind the top of his desk.

"I'm afraid a plagiarist can't ever become a Young Pioneer, not ever, not even in the fourth grade or the fifth. Igor has betrayed our trust. How can a plagiarist wear a red Young Pioneer's tie and salute our red flag with the words 'always ready'? Can we trust a plagiarist to be 'always ready' to defend our country?"

42

"No," we all replied in glum voices.

"And of course," said the teacher, "a plagiarist cannot be the winner of our contest. The winner is..." She looked at the class for a second, deciding who the new winner was going to be.

"The winner is — Anya Pamakova."

Anya P. sat at her desk, pink and proud, with her nose in the air. The teacher made all of us clap our hands and cheer Anya. Only I, my best friend Lena M., and a few others who were Igor's friends didn't cheer.

I whispered to Lena, "I'm sure she was the one who told the teacher about the cartoon on TV."

I was right. When everybody was done clapping and cheering, the teacher said:

"Anya Pamakova is not only a good story writer, but she also has the dutiful heart of a Young Pioneer. It is thanks to her that we know the truth and have learned our lesson: Plagiarism Never Again."

I listened to the teacher, feeling uneasy; I didn't think what Igor had done was very bad. Anyway, I was glad the teacher hadn't promised *me* the red necktie that she took away from Igor, because I could see Igor was very angry about it.

BUG

A few days later, I had chewing gum for the second time. Ten months had gone by since I'd been on the beach with Karl and Monika. Now my aunt sent some chewing gum for me and my brother from behind the border.

Misha chewed it for a while, then took it out of his mouth and rolled it into a little ball. He said to me, "Tomorrow I'll take it to school and trade it for stamps." He had a stamp collection, and so did two of his friends. Never before had his friends seen chewing gum. They didn't know he'd already chewed this gum, and they traded him some stamps for it.

A few days later, I thought I would try to follow his

example. I rolled my chewing gum into a smooth little ball and took it to school. In the hall, I saw Igor Levov. He still looked unhappy about what the teacher had said to him about his story. Because I felt sorry for Igor, I decided to give him the chewing gum as a present.

He put the gum into his mouth and started chewing. I looked at him. When the opening bell rang, he took it out of his mouth and rolled it into the same smooth little ball as before. At that moment he understood the secret, that I had given him a piece of used chewing gum. But he didn't seem to mind. He said, "I bet I could trade this for something!" and he cheered up a little bit. We decided that we'd walk into his sister's fifth-grade class during lunch and try to make a trade for the gum.

I waited for Igor in the hall at lunchtime. He walked into the classroom and started showing the chewing gum to the big kids. I saw two of them come up to Igor. One was holding something. He held it out to Igor, but Igor didn't want to take it. He grabbed Igor's arm, then took away his chewing gum and put the thing into his hand.

"Don't look, or you'll scream," Igor told me, back out in the hall. He was so pale. He was holding something. It was a bug that had been stuck with a pin; it was still wriggling. I did feel like screaming.

We started walking back to our class.

"What are we going to do with it now?" Igor asked me.

"We've got to get rid of it," I replied. "Can't we give it to somebody?"

"Let's show it to Anya. I bet she'll scream!" I guess he hated her then, and I was on his side.

She was sitting at her desk in the classroom. The

teacher was away. I went up to her and said, "Here, Anya, look at this!" When Anya saw what was on the pin Igor was holding, her eyes got very big for a second, and then she screamed so loud I wished I could shut my ears.

"You're supposed to be the first Young Pioneer in our class," said Igor to Anya. "A Pioneer should be brave. How come you're screaming?" Anya didn't say anything; she was crying.

The bell rang, and Igor threw the bug out the window. I always felt bad about scaring Anya that time, even though I thought she deserved it.

PAVLIK MOROZOV

The first story we read in second grade, just after we had learned to read well, was about Pavlik Morozov. All three second-grade sections participated in a discussion about him.

"Pavlik Morozov was a real hero even though he was just a young boy," our teacher said. "What was it that made him a hero?" she asked us. Anya Pamakova raised her hand.

"Because he told on his parents," she said.

"Why did he tell on his parents? Didn't he love them?" asked the teacher.

Many hands shot up. "His parents were bad. They

were kulaks, and you can't really love kulaks, even if they're your parents. It's shameful to love them more than the motherland." Again it was Anya who spoke.

"Who can tell us what they were, these kulaks?"

"They were rich peasants, and everybody else was poor. They had money and the others didn't; that's why they were bad," said Anya.

"Very good, Anya," the teacher replied, praising her.

Anya looked just the way a good student was supposed to look: she rested her arms on top of her desk, right arm on left, and she held her head very straight. When she wanted to answer a question, she didn't stretch and shake her arm in the air, as the rest of us did; she raised her arm slowly until her elbow was on the desk and her fingers pointed up. I thought that was why the teacher chose Anya, again and again, to answer the important questions.

Sitting there, looking at Anya, hearing the teacher praise her, I thought that maybe Anya was a little bit like Pavlik Morozov. Pavlik Morozov became a hero because he told on his father. The militiamen came and took his father away.

"Why did Pavlik Morozov do that?" I asked my mother later that day.

"Do what?" My mother didn't know what I was talking about.

I told her the story. "I think I know why he told on his parents," I said. "He's like Anya Pamakova. She wants to be praised, so she raises her hand just the way the teacher told us."

"Why don't you, too, raise your hand the way the teacher told you?"

"That's what I was going to ask you about, Mama!

Should I be like Pavlik Morozov and Anya?"

"What has Anya got to do with Pavlik Morozov?" my mother asked.

"Well, Anya raises her hand that special way because she wants to be praised. And Pavlik Morozov betrayed his parents because he wanted to become a hero and wanted everybody to praise him, and to know about him so many years after it happened! Do you really want me to be like that, Mama?"

"Of course I don't want you to be like *that*, Nina," my mother said. "But I think what Pavlik Morozov did was very different from what Anya does. Did Pavlik love his father at all? Did he miss him after the men arrested his father and sent him away to Siberia? When Pavlik learned about his father's death, far from home, was he sorry he informed on his own father? I hope he *was* sorry. And of course I hope that

you, Ninotchka, would never do what Pavlik Morozov did. First, because we're not *kulaks;* second,
because —"

"Because I wouldn't want to! Because I love you!" I
ran up to my mother to embrace her. Tears were
streaming down my cheeks.

"I know you love me, and I'm happy that you don't
want to be like Pavlik Morozov," my mother said,
stroking my hair and kissing the top of my head. "As
for raising your hand in class the way your teacher
taught you..."

"You don't know about Anya!" I said. "It's not just
that she raises her hand in class — it's that she tells on
people! Like she told the teacher about Igor's white
mouse story from TV! So she's really like Pavlik Morozov, don't you see that?"

"Sh-sh," said my mother, kissing my forehead. "If

you don't want to raise your hand that special way your teacher likes, then don't. I'm proud of you just the way you are!"

The next day the teacher told us to write our first composition. We had to write a whole page to answer the question "What would you have done in Pavlik Morozov's place?" When we'd discussed it the day before, everybody said that Pavlik Morozov was right, that our Soviet state depended on people like Pavlik, and that each of us would have done the same if his or her parents were the shame of our Soviet motherland. That's the word they used: a shame. It was our teacher's word, and everybody repeated it.

I started writing: *I'm not like Pavlik Morozov. I love my parents more than anything else in the whole world. I don't think I could tell on my—*

I peeked into the notebook of my neighbor, Lena M.

She was writing: *I hope I can be as brave as Pavlik Morozov.*

I nudged Igor Levov in the seat in front of me. I wanted to see what he was writing. He showed me: *I admire Pavlik Morozov. Maybe he loved his parents, but the motherland must come first. I wish I could be as strong as he.*

Then I crossed out what I'd been writing, tore that page from my notebook, crumpled it up, and started over again: *I think Pavlik Morozov was right. I want to be like him. If my parents do something wrong, I'll know: it's them or our Soviet motherland. And I'll choose our Soviet motherland. Because my parents love only me and my brother, and our Soviet state cares for all.*

I felt very bad about what I was writing. But everybody was writing that way, even my friends. Are they writing what they really think, I wondered. Or was I the only one who loved my parents more than anything else in the world, even more than our Soviet state?

When I finished writing, I shook my fountain pen in the air, and an ink spot landed right in the middle of the page. It covered Pavlik's last name, so only the first letter, *M*, showed. I knew the teacher wouldn't like it, but I didn't care. If I had to write falsely, it was better if the page looked ugly, full of inkblots and bad handwriting.

I didn't tell my parents about my composition. I decided I would show them that I loved them more than anything by simply not giving them any worries. And for that I had to do really well in school, so my teacher would say good things about me to my mother and father at the next parents' meeting. I even started raising my hand in that special way, elbow on the table, fingers pointing up, as our teacher had taught us. So what if Anya raised hers like that? I did it because I loved my parents, not because I was like Anya or like Pavlik Morozov. I wasn't a traitor like them. No matter what I wrote in that composition.

A QUEEN OF TIME

My father was allowed to go behind the border a couple of times, to visit his sister in England. I missed him when he went away. When he came back, I was happy. He brought back all sorts of interesting things. I didn't tell kids in my class that my father went behind the border. I knew that their parents couldn't travel to other places, and I didn't like to brag about my father. I didn't want them to think my family was any different from other families.

After one trip he brought me a watch. It was a real watch; it ticked, it showed the time. And it was all mine. It fit my wrist perfectly. I wore it all day Saturday and Sunday, but I would not wear it to school: I didn't want the other children to know that my father could get me things their fathers couldn't. I didn't want to be different. But even though I never took it to school, my friends soon learned about my watch. They admired it. They watched its two hands move. They asked me to let them wear it for a while.

After my watch was no longer a secret, I started wearing it every day. Soon everyone in my class knew about it. Everyone wanted to sit next to me and look at my watch, but they couldn't all sit at my table. Instead, they would turn their heads, look at me, and point at their own, empty wrists. In this way they could silently ask me how much time was left till the end of class. I would consult my watch and hold up five fingers for five minutes or ten fingers for ten minutes.

The teacher used to praise me for being a good student. But now when I wore my watch to class, I didn't hear much of what the teacher said. I was too busy counting minutes.

One day the principal came into our class, four minutes before recess, and saw me holding up four fingers. She walked over to my desk and asked where I had gotten the watch. When the principal talked to me, I was always too frightened to answer. "Her father brought it from behind the border," the teacher said.

The principal made me hand her my watch and stand up. She put her hand on my shoulder. "Not long ago, this child was one of our best students," she said. "What happened to Nina K.? Why did her grades get worse? Why did she stop listening in class? Now we know."

The principal held up my watch for everyone to see. "This," she said, "is what capitalists use to spoil our Soviet children. They have special factories where they make watches for kids. When those watches get into a child's hands, that child changes from a good child to a bad one. She no longer studies. She feels she's better than others. She feels special, because she has something the other children don't have. But deep down she doesn't like being special. She likes being just like everybody else. Don't you, Nina?"

I could only nod my head. Something in my throat wouldn't let me speak. Tears were streaming down my cheeks.

After that, I stopped wearing my watch to school. Now I was just like everybody else, watchless. But I missed the days when everyone turned to me and asked me the time. I had brought smiles to my friends' faces when I held up three fingers: only three minutes to lunch. And I had made them sigh when I held up all ten fingers twice: twenty minutes, uh-oh, too long. In those days I felt like a queen of time. Now I was only a good student.

IN RED SQUARE

Red Square is the most beautiful place in Moscow; it's on all the postcards. Lenin's tomb is there, and other important buildings. I went to Red Square many times with my parents. On my first visit I expected to see everything red: red buildings, red ground. But almost nothing on that famous square was actually red.

I asked Misha, "Why isn't Red Square red?"

He thought for a little while, then said, "Maybe because it's so old, the red has just faded away."

I wondered why nobody painted it red again. I remembered two painters who came to our school to paint the fence around the playground; at one time the fence had been blue, but then the paint became old and chipped. They made it nice and blue all over again.

Well, if nobody had thought of doing that for Red Square, it would have to be me.

The following day I said to Lena M., "Lena, next time I go to Red Square, you come with me."

"Why?" she asked.

"You see, Red Square is so old that all the red paint has worn off. We'll take our watercolors and our brushes. We'll paint Red Square."

"Do you think we are allowed to do that?"

"That doesn't matter," I said. "The government will thank us for it later. If nobody thought of it till now, it's got to be us."

"But how will we do it?" she asked.

"You just stand guard and hold the paint. Look around and tell me if anyone's coming. I'll do the rest," I said bravely.

I talked my brother into taking me and Lena to Red Square the following Sunday. I didn't tell him about my plan because I wasn't sure he'd like it. When the day arrived, Lena came to our apartment with a big bag full of watercolors and some brushes.

The square was full of people. Visitors from other countries were standing in groups, listening to a guide. My brother asked me if I wanted to go to the museum there or to look at Lenin in his tomb. "No," I said, "Lena and I just want to stand here and watch."

"Okay," Misha said, "but don't go anywhere. I'll come back for you in half an hour."

"Let's start there, Lena." I pointed to the end of the square, where there weren't so many people. We walked over and took out our watercolors and brushes. We put the paints and water jar on the ground. I kneeled with a brush in my hand, while Lena stood with her legs and arms apart so people wouldn't see me.

But they saw anyway. Soon a crowd gathered around us, and it grew larger and larger. The people spoke in many languages. Only once in a while did I hear some Russian words. We didn't pay any attention to the crowd. Since they already saw us, Lena didn't have to stand like a guard, so she knelt down next to me and helped me paint.

"Maybe watercolor isn't the right paint," Lena whispered to me. Somebody must have understood her, because we were handed a jar of a different kind of red paint. Our work went along much better with that new paint. Every time we finished coloring a flagstone, people applauded.

Suddenly we heard a new, loud voice: "What is going on here?" We looked up and saw two militiamen making their way through the crowd. They came over to us and picked up our paints, brushes, and bag.

"Hooliganism in Red Square is strictly forbidden," one of them said to us.

"Go away!" the other ordered the crowd. The people began to leave.

"Your name, address, name of parents, please." The first militiaman took out a pen and a notebook.

"Are we being arrested?" asked Lena.

"First you tell us where you live," said the second man.

Then we heard a familiar voice. "They're with me! They're with me!" It was my brother. Misha was running toward us, looking very worried. He took my hand and Lena's and asked, "What happened?"

"We were only trying to paint the Red Square red," I said.

The militiamen wrote down our address and let us

go. Soon we were home. My mother grumbled, "Where do you get these crazy ideas, Ninotchka? Why do you want to paint Red Square red? What is the matter with you?"

"But, Mama, why is it called Red Square if it's not really red?"

"Because *krasnaya* doesn't really mean 'red,'" my father said. "Many years ago it meant 'beautiful'— *krasivaya*."

"I'm afraid you will have a difficult life," my mother sighed. "You are too independent for your own good, Ninotchka."

I thought painting the square was good. I thought being independent was good. But what was my own good, I wondered.

SECRETS

My school was far away from home. When I was in kindergarten two years earlier, my father used to take me there by trolley bus. Now Dora Mihailovna, my baby-sitter, took me to school by streetcar. I liked Dora Mihailovna, and I missed her when she was not there. After school we'd go shopping for my mother. We stood in one long line for butter, in another long line for meat, and in yet another long line for vegetables. Most people looked tired and bored standing in line; but I liked it, because while we stood there, Dora Mihailovna told me stories.

One time we stood in a very long line, and when our turn came, Dora Mihailovna couldn't find the purse with the money. It was a purse my mother had given her. She searched her bag and her pockets, but it wasn't there. She looked pale; I thought she might start to cry.

"How can I look into your mother's eyes if I've lost her money?" she said. "What will she think?" I didn't know what to say. I was hoping my mother wouldn't be angry with her.

"What if she thinks I stole that money?"

"I will say that you didn't, Dora Mihailovna! I'm sure my mother won't be angry then." But I really wasn't too sure. I had no idea what my mother would think or say. Maybe she'd get somebody else to take me to school and do the shopping. I knew I didn't want anyone but Dora Mihailovna to take me to school. If my parents get another baby-sitter, I thought, I won't go to school at all.

But we shouldn't have worried. When my mother

learned what happened, she believed us and didn't say anything bad.

There was another time I was very afraid for Dora Mihailovna. One day, when my parents were at work and Dora Mihailovna was dusting a shelf, she overturned my father's radio. She picked it up, turned it on,...but not a sound came out of it. "That's it," she said in a sad, quiet voice. "When your father learns about this..."

"Dora Mihailovna," I said, "I'll say I did it. Then he won't be angry at you."

"Thank you, Ninotchka, but I don't want you to lie, even if it's to help me out. We must always tell the truth. Even if your father gets angry and will not let me work for your family again, it's better than telling a lie."

She left a note for my father saying she'd broken the radio while she was dusting the shelf. She wrote that she was very sorry, but what could she do now except be honest about it? Then she finished dusting the shelf, warmed up some chicken soup for me, and when I finished eating it, she left.

I tried to do my homework, but I kept thinking about the note and what would happen. My father would come back from work and see the note, and then what would he do, without his radio? This radio was his life. Every day after dinner, he would listen to it for hours. He listened only to one station — the BBC. It was a special station: it came from behind the border. My father wanted to know what was going on in the world. He listened to the BBC news, he used to say, because our Soviet radio stations and newspapers never told what was *really* happening in the world.

Because the BBC came from behind the border, it was hard to hear. The voice of the BBC announcer came out thin and weak. My father said it was hard to hear not because it was so far away, but because the Soviet radio "jammed" the BBC, covered it up with noise on purpose, to keep people from listening to it. He would turn the radio this way and that, or he would lower it to the floor, then hold it up in the air — anything to make the voice of the BBC come through. "In this country you can know the truth about the world only if you listen to the BBC. That's why I have to do this, Ninotchka," he would say, holding the radio up or striking its top with his fist. We called this "hitting the BBC."

He never turned the radio up loud, and he always checked to see that all the windows and doors were closed, because he didn't want our neighbors to know he was listening to the BBC. Those three letters were our secret. My brother and I could not mention them in school or with our friends. I used to be afraid I would suddenly say "BBC" just like that, when nobody asked me anything. I would sit in class and, instead of listening to the teacher, think about the BBC and feel that I knew something that nobody else did. My secret would make me feel different from everyone else. Then I'd hear the teacher's voice: "What are you daydreaming about, Nina K.?"

"About the... Nothing." I always held my tongue in time. At night I used to have bad dreams about my parents getting arrested for listening to the forbidden station.

So when Dora Mihailovna broke the radio, I was both happy and unhappy. My father wouldn't be listening to the BBC anymore, so there would be no more secret, and I wouldn't have to be afraid of blurting out those three forbidden letters in school. I was tired of carrying that secret around. But if Dora Mihailovna got into trouble for breaking the radio, I wouldn't be happy at all. This radio was my father's treasure.

What if he gets so upset that he tells Dora Mihailovna never to come to our house again, I thought. Who will take me to school? Who will take me along shopping on the way home? Who will tell me stories while we wait in the lines for eggs or butter?

I thought maybe I should hide Dora Mihailovna's note and tell my father that *I* had broken the radio. Then instead of the BBC secret, I'd have another one, the secret of the hidden note, and I knew Dora Mihailovna didn't want me to do that for her. While I was trying to decide what to do, the time passed and my father came home.

But nothing happened. He read Dora Mihailovna's note, and he wasn't angry. My father said he trusted her; anyone could have dropped the radio. He got it fixed and went on listening to the BBC every evening, just as before. And I still had that secret with me. Every morning I still had to remind myself not to blurt out "BBC" in school. It made me happy, though, to know that my parents trusted Dora Mihailovna as much as I did. Until I was big enough to go to school on my own, she and I rode the streetcar every morning and every afternoon. While we stood in long lines for groceries, she told me stories about when she was a little girl; and while she was telling me stories, I could forget my BBC secret that was so hard to carry around.

PERMISSION TO LEAVE

The spring when I was eleven was a difficult time. Something was happening at home, in my family, that I didn't know anything about. Something terrible, and it had to do with my mother, my father, my brother, and myself. During the day everything was as usual: my mother was at work, my father was preparing for his evening teaching job. Yet I knew that something secretive was going on, and that at night, when my parents were sure I was asleep in my room, they went into the kitchen and discussed their secret again.

Each night I only pretended to go to sleep for a few minutes; then I rolled off my bed, tiptoed to the kitchen, and listened in — crouching behind the door, noiselessly jumping back every time the door started to open. I was terrified by what I heard. Every time I tip-toed back to my room, I kneeled in front of my bed and in a whisper begged some strong, superior being to stop my parents from carrying out their plan.

That spring my friend Lena M. and I were elected class representatives on our school council. We were happy because the whole 4B class had voted for us. I knew everybody wanted to be friends with Lena M., but I wasn't sure all those kids liked me, too. We couldn't wait till that first Monday in May when we would go to the school council for the first time. But something very different happened that day.

Irina Rodionovna, our homeroom teacher, stopped me on my way out of class after third period and said, "I want you to wait for me after classes are over today. You and I must have a talk."

I wanted to say that I couldn't, that I had to go to the school council after classes were over, that this was such an important day for Lena and me! But she was out in the hall already, talking to the third-grade teacher from the class next door, and I was afraid to interrupt.

When classes were over, I waited for Irina Rodionovna near her desk. She pointed at the corner of the classroom, where we had hung our class newspaper and posters the week before. I was the editor of the newspaper, so I didn't mind sitting next to it.

"America! Your family is going away to America!" Irina Rodionovna said.

That was the secret my parents talked about late each night behind the closed door of our kitchen. That was the plan I was so afraid they'd carry out. To leave Russia! What could be more terrible than that?

But to hear my teacher talk about our leaving was more terrible! "The Soviet Union gave you a free education. Now you're going to use it in another country, Russia's enemy, against Russia. You're a traitor."

I stared at the floor.

"And what language will you speak in America, anyway, traitor?" she asked.

"I'll speak English there," I said.

"You don't know it well enough," she said.

"You're the one who taught it to us," I mumbled.

"Your father will die of a heart attack in the plane on the way there. That's how traitors die," she said.

I didn't say anything. I was crying.

"Jews were killing Russian children during the Great Patriotic War. They're the cause of our country's misfortune!"

"I don't believe that!" I sobbed. "Show me a history

book that says so." I knew that everything she told me then was a lie.

She attacked me and I defended myself. I defended my parents' decision to leave Russia for America, even though the word *traitor*, repeated so many times, hit me like a fist in my stomach, again and again.

When Irina Rodionovna finally let me go, Lena M. was waiting for me in the hall. "Too bad you couldn't come," she said, running up to me. "The council meeting was great!" She even jumped when she said it — that's how happy she was to be the class representative. Then she looked at me more closely. "What happened to you? Why are you crying?"

On the way home, sobbing, I told Lena what happened. I said that my parents were going to America, and that even though I couldn't bear to think or talk about leaving Russia, I didn't mind it so much after this terrible talk with Irina Rodionovna. In the streetcar I repeated the things I'd heard my parents say: that my grandfather was shot by Stalin when my mother was a young girl and my grandmother spent five years in a labor camp because she was the wife of an "enemy of the people"; that neither of them was guilty of anything; they were just like the millions of other innocent people who had been arrested and shot.... I wasn't sure exactly what all these things meant, but I'd heard my parents discuss them often, especially behind the closed kitchen door. I knew our leaving the country had something to do with these things. Lena consoled me as I sobbed, and people in the streetcar turned their heads to see who was talking so loudly about these forbidden subjects.

At home my parents told me they'd received a call from the principal. She said that tomorrow they were going to take away my red Young Pioneer's tie at a special ceremony in front of the whole school.

"How did the school learn about our going away to America?" my mother wondered. "How is it possible? We haven't told anyone — we haven't even applied for permission to leave yet!"

"In our country, informers travel faster than one's own imagination," my father said. "Don't worry, Ninotchka. You won't be going to school tomorrow — or the day after," he added. "They're just trying to frighten us into staying when they talk about taking off your red tie. Tie or no tie, it won't matter, if we get our permission to leave.... But if we don't..."

My father stood there, his hands in his pockets, looking at the three of us: my mother, my brother, and me. What would happen to us if we didn't get permission? Would they take off my red tie in front of the whole school and call me a traitor again?

From that day on, I no longer crouched behind the kitchen door at night. And now when I fell asleep, I had the same wish as my parents: to get a permit to leave, as soon as possible. To emigrate.

NOTES

SOVIET UNION; RUSSIA

The Union of Soviet Socialist Republics (often called the U.S.S.R. or the Soviet Union) existed from 1922 until 1991. There were fifteen republics: Armenia, Azerbaijan, Byelorussia, Estonia, Georgia, Kazakhstan, Kirghizia, Latvia, Lithuania, Moldavia, Russia, Tajikistan, Turkmenistan, Ukraine, and Uzbekistan. In 1991 the union was disbanded, and now there are fifteen independent nations instead of one huge empire.

Russia was the largest republic, and Russian was the official language of the entire union. The people in every republic had to learn Russian in addition to their own language. Moscow, the largest city in Russia, was the capital of the Soviet Union. People from many different republics lived there, but mostly it was a city of Russians.

COMMUNISM; CAPITALISM

In February 1917 the first Russian Revolution overthrew the rule of the czar and the nobility. For several months Russia had a provisional government that had democratic aims. In October 1917 the second Russian Revolution (also known as the October or Bolshevik revolution) violently overthrew the provisional government. It brought about the end of a capitalist system of private ownership in Russia and the beginnings of Communist rule. There was then only one political party, the Communist party. People who thought differently from the government were punished.

Communists blamed capitalists for all the things that were wrong in the world and in Russia. They were against a few capitalists owning most of the country's wealth and the division of people into the very rich and the very poor. In 1917 they proclaimed that from then on, workers and peasants would be in sole charge of their country and their lives. Factories, businesses, farms, houses, and other important things were taken away from their owners, who were all considered capitalists, and given to the government. The government was supposed to make sure that everyone worked equally hard and had an equal share in all profits.

In 1945, at the end of World War II (which Russians called the Great Patriotic War), much of the world was divided into the capitalist nations, such as the United States and the countries of Western Europe, and the Communist countries of Eastern Europe, the Soviet Union, China, and several others. The capitalist nations were afraid that Communists would take over more countries, and the Communists believed the capitalists would do the same. The Cold War, a period of hostility between members of the two systems, lasted for nearly fifty years.

In Communist countries, capitalists were talked about as greedy people whose only goal in life was to have more and more of other people's money, to live well while other people broke their backs working for them. No one was supposed to rest while others worked, and everyone was supposed to be equal; but they weren't. A few privileged "important" people got the best housing, the best food, and luxuries of all sorts. Most citizens, though, lived in cramped apartments, shopped in stores that often lacked the most necessary products, and had to wait in very long, separate lines to buy everything from bread to toilet paper to clothing. Communism seemed like an attractive idea, but it didn't work out so well in practice.

LENIN

Vladimir Lenin is considered the organizer of the Russian Revolution. He was the Soviet Union's first leader and the head of the Communist party. Pictures of him were everywhere: in schools, in hospitals, in post offices, in the streets. When Lenin died in 1924, he was not buried like other people. His body was preserved and people came from all over the country to look at him. All children used to read stories about Lenin's childhood and sing songs about him. To many people, he was like a saint or a god.

KULAKS

About ten years after the October revolution, many farmers were accused of having too much wealth and refusing to give it to the state. The government called these people "kulaks." *Kulak* is used to mean "tight-fisted, greedy"; the word literally means "fist." Hundreds of thousands of farmers were arrested by the government and sent away to Siberia, one of the coldest and harshest regions of the Soviet Union, where many of them died.

RUSSIAN JEWS

Although anti-Semitism had existed in Russia for a long time, under communism all religions, including Judaism, were banned. The government in the Soviet Union said that Jews were not real Russians, that they were a different nationality— even families that had lived there for generations. Many people were unfriendly to them; Jews were made to feel different from everyone else, even though they spoke the same language and did all the same kinds of things as everyone else. After 1975, many Jews who received permission left Russia in the hope of finding a better life elsewhere.

SOVIET NEWS, CENSORSHIP, AND THE BBC

Soviet news reports didn't always tell the truth about what was going on in the world. Radio, television, and the newspapers were all controlled by the government, and people only learned about what the government wanted them to know. Americans were always shown as bad, and nothing good about capitalist countries could get into the news. There were very few foreigners in Russia, and the government did not allow ordinary Soviet citizens to have contact with them.

People who wanted to find out about what was going on in the world had to listen to radio stations from other countries, such as the BBC (British Broadcasting Corporation). Most people were afraid to do this, because it could make the government suspicious and they could be arrested and sent away.

STALIN; ARRESTS; LABOR CAMPS

In 1937, the most terrible year in Soviet history, millions of innocent people died under the dictatorship of Joseph Stalin. Even though many of them sincerely believed in communism and the good it would bring, they were called "enemies of the people" and were arrested and killed. Many others were sent away to spend years in prisons or labor camps where they were starved or tortured to death. After the death of Stalin in 1953, the Soviet government said those people were innocent and shouldn't have been killed. But for years people still lived in fear of being arrested for saying or doing something wrong.

RED SQUARE

Red Square is in the center of Moscow, along the Moscow River. It is hundreds of years old. The Kremlin, which is beside Red Square, takes up more than sixty acres and has several cathedrals and palaces as well as administrative buildings. The Soviet government met there. The beautiful St. Basil's cathedral, as well as Lenin's tomb, is on Red Square. Soviet leaders made speeches from the top of Lenin's tomb, and military parades took place in the square just below.

It is not because the Soviet flag was red that the square is called Red Square. In Russian as it was spoken at the time Red Square was constructed, the same word meant both "red" and "beautiful." Long before the revolution, public executions made the square bloody, and the name changed in people's minds from Beautiful Square to Red Square.

YOUNG OCTOBRISTS AND YOUNG PIONEERS

The Soviet government had Communist groups for all ages. In the first grade, all children in the Soviet Union became Young Octobrists. The name *Octobrists* comes from the month of the Bolshevik revolution. Third or fourth graders became Young Pioneers. Later, in the seventh or eighth grade, students became members of the Komsomol, which comes from the Russian words for "Communist Union of Youth." A person might stay in the Komsomol until he or she was twenty-five or twenty-seven, and then might join the Communist party itself.

SOVIET SCHOOLS

In the Soviet Union, kindergarten was not part of elementary school. Soviet children went to kindergarten from age three to age seven. When they were seven years old, they started first grade. Thus, Soviet first graders were the age that most American second graders are. Soviet schools were not divided into elementary, junior high, and high school; all the grades were in one building. Also, instead of twelve grades as American schools have, there were only ten.

NINA KOSSMAN was born in Moscow, Russia, in 1959. After emigrating to the United States with her family in 1973, she earned her B.A. in literature from Bennington College and a master's degree in Russian literature from the University of Pittsburgh. Her writing, which has been published in several countries, includes a collection of her poetry published in Moscow in 1990 and *In the Inmost Hour of the Soul*, her translation of the poetry of Marina Tsvetayeva. Ms. Kossman is also an award-winning painter and has taught languages to both children and adults. She lives in New York.

Best in biography and autobiography from
BEECH TREE BOOKS

Anne Frank: Life in Hiding
by Johanna Hurwitz

Anonymously Yours
by Richard Peck

But I'll Be Back Again
by Cynthia Rylant

Dear Dr. Bell . . . Your Friend, Helen Keller
by Judith St. George

E. B. White: Some Writer!
by Beverly Gherman

Harriet: The Life and World of Harriet Beecher Stowe
by Norma Johnston

In Kindling Flame: The Story of Hannah Senesh, 1921–1944
by Linda Atkinson

The Invisible Thread
by Yoshiko Uchida

The Life and Death of Martin Luther King, Jr.
by James Haskins

The Lost Garden
by Laurence Yep

Louisa May: The World and Works of Louisa May Alcott
by Norma Johnston

The Moon & I
by Betsy Byars

The Road from Home: The Story of an Armenian Girl
by David Kherdian